# KIDS ON EARTH

*Wildlife Adventures – Explore The World*
*Clouded Leopard-Cambodia*

Sensei Paul David

# COPYRIGHT PAGE

Kids On Earth: Wildlife Adventures - Explore The World

Clouded Leopard- Cambodia

by Sensei Paul David,

Copyright © 2023.

All rights reserved.

978-1-77848-211-3

KoE_WildLife_Amazon_PaperbackBook_cambodia_clouded leopard

978-1-77848-210-6 KoE_WildLife_Amazon_eBook_cambodia_clouded leopard

978-1-77848-408-7 KoE_Wildlife_CloudedLeopard_Ingram_PaperbackBook

This book is not authorized for free distribution copying.

www.senseipublishing.com

@senseipublishing
#senseipublishing

## Synopsis

This book explores the unique traits and habitats of the clouded leopard, an endangered species found in the forests of Southeast Asia, including Cambodia. It looks at the clouded leopard's strength, agility, diet, and behaviour, as well as 30 unique and interesting facts about this incredible big cat. Through this book, readers can learn more about the clouded leopard, as well as why it is important to protect this species.

# Get Our FREE eBooks Now!

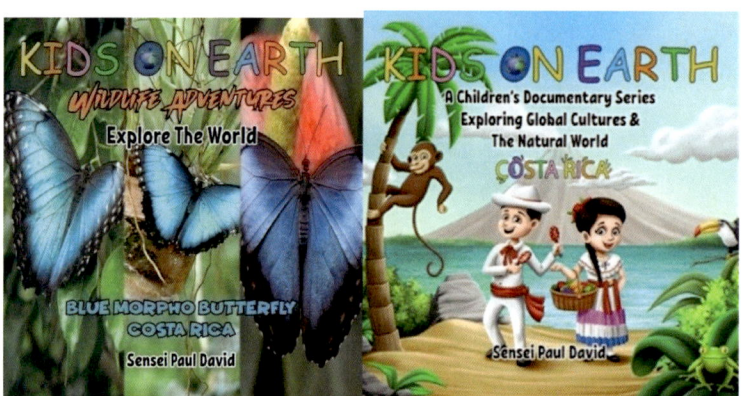

kidsonearth.life    kidsonearth.world

# Click Below for Another Book In Each Series

senseipublishing.com/KoE_SERIES
senseipublishing.com/KoE_Wildlife_SERIES

## KoE EnEspañol

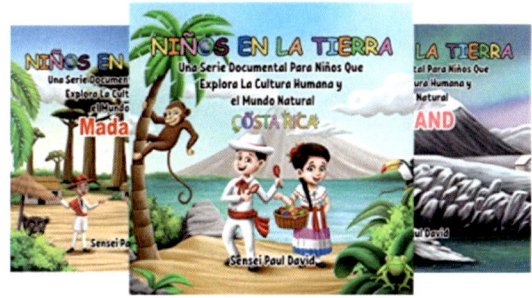

senseipublishing.com/KoE_SERIES_SPANISH

www.senseipublishing.com

# Join Our Publishing Journey!

If you would like to receive FUTURE FREE BOOKS and get to know us better, please click www.senseipublishing.com and join our newsletter by entering your email address in the pop-up box.

**Follow Our Blog: senseipauldavid.ca**

Follow/Like/Subscribe: Facebook, Instagram, YouTube: @senseipublishing

Scan the QR Code with your phone or tablet to follow us on social media:

Like / Subscribe / Follow

# Introduction

Welcome to the amazing world of the clouded leopard!

This book is full of fun facts the incredible species of big cat are found in the forests of Southeast Asia, including Cambodia. Also, we'll explore the unique traits and habitsthe clouded leopard, as well as some incredible facts about

The clouded leopard is a medium-sized cat, with a head-body length of 90-100 cm (2.9-3.3 ft) and a tail length of about 70 cm (2.3 ft).

The clouded leopard is a solitary animal and prefers to avoid contact with other animals.

The clouded leopard is an excellent climber and can leap up to nine meters in a single jump.

It has a long tail that can be used for balance when climbing trees.

It is a nocturnal animal and is most active at night.

The clouded leopard's coat is usually greyish-brown with black spots, called "clouds", which give it its name.

The clouded leopard is a carnivore and its diet consists of small mammals, birds, and reptiles.

It has an amazing sense of smell and uses it to hunt prey.

The clouded leopard is found in the forests and jungles of Southeast Asia, including parts of India, China, and Cambodia.

The clouded leopard is an endangered species and its population is decreasing due to loss of habitat and hunting.

The clouded leopard is a shy animal and will rarely interact with humans unless provoked.

It is an excellent swimmer and can easily swim across a river.

The clouded leopard can have up to five cubs in a single litter.

The clouded leopard has a loud and distinctive call that can be heard up to two kilometers away.

The clouded leopard is an ambush predator and will often wait in trees until its prey passes by.

The clouded leopard is an excellent hunter and can take down prey much larger than itself, such as deer and wild pigs.

The clouded leopard has a long lifespan, with some living up to 20 years in the wild.

399

The clouded leopard is an incredibly fast and agile animal and can move at speeds of up to 50 kilometers per hour.

The clouded leopard has a very strong sense of hearing and can detect the slightest movements and sounds.

The clouded leopard is an expert hunter and can leap up to five times its own body length to catch its prey.

The clouded leopard has a unique tongue that is used to groom its fur.

The clouded leopard is an endangered species due to habitat loss and hunting.

The clouded leopard is an excellent tree climber and can often be seen on branches in the forest.

The clouded leopard is an excellent tree climber and can often be seen on branches in the forest.

## Conclusion

The clouded leopard is an amazing animal with some incredible traits and abilities. It is a solitary animal that is found in the forests of Southeast Asia, including Cambodia. It is an endangered species due to habitat loss and hunting, but with conservation efforts, we can help protect this amazing big cat.

# Thank you for reading this book!

If you found this book helpful, I would be grateful if you would **post an honest review on Amazon** so this book can reach other supportive readers like you!

All you need to do is digitally flip to the back and leave your review. Or visit amazon.com/author/senseipauldavid click the correct book cover and click on the blue link next to the yellow stars that say, "Customer reviews."

*As always…*

*It's a great day to be alive!*

# Get/Share Our FREE eBooks Now!

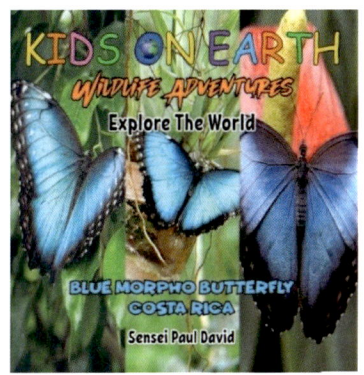 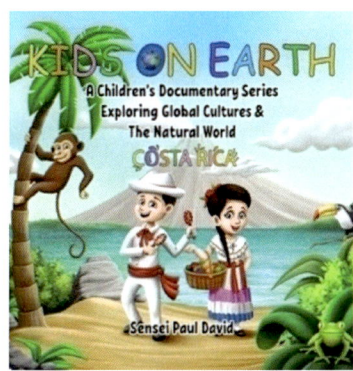

[kidsonearth.life](kidsonearth.life)  　　　　　[kidsonearth.world](kidsonearth.world)

# Click Below for Another Book In Each Series

senseipublishing.com/KoE_SERIES senseipublishing.com/KoE_Wildlife_SERIES

## KoE EnEspañol

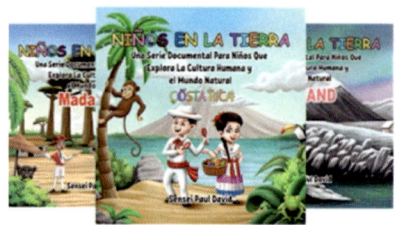

senseipublishing.com/KoE_SERIES_SPANISH

[www.senseipublishing.com](www.senseipublishing.com)

www.senseipublishing.com

@senseipublishing
#senseipublishing

Check out our **recommendations** for other books for adults & kids plus other great resources by visiting
www.senseipublishing.com/resources/

# Join Our Publishing Journey!

If you would like to receive FREE BOOKS and special offers, please visit www.senseipublishing.com and join our newsletter by entering your email address in the pop-up box

## Follow Our Engaging Blog NOW!

## senseipauldavid.ca

## Get Our FREE Books Today!

Click & Share the Links Below

### FREE Kids Books
lifeofbailey.senseipublishing.com
kidsonearth.senseipublishing.com
### FREE Self-Development Book

senseiselfdevelopment.senseipublishing.com

**FREE BONUS!!!**
**Experience Over 25 FREE Engaging Guided Meditations!**

Prized Skills & Practices for Adults & Kids. Help Restore Deep Sleep, Lower Stress, Improve Posture, Navigate Uncertainty & More.

Download the Free Insight Timer App and click the link below:
http://insig.ht/sensei_paul

# About Sensei Publishing

Sensei Publishing commits itself to help people of all ages transform into better versions of themselves by providing high-quality and research-based self-development books with an emphasis on mental health and guided meditations. Sensei Publishing offers well-written e-books, audiobooks, paperbacks, and online courses that simplify complicated but practical topics in line with its mission to inspire people toward positive transformation.

It's a great day to be alive!

# About the Author

I create simple & transformative eBooks & Guided Meditations for Adults & Children proven to help navigate uncertainty, solve niche problems & bring families closer together.

I'm a former finance project manager, private pilot, jiu-jitsu instructor, musician & former University of Toronto Fitness Trainer. I prefer a science-based approach to focus on these & other areas in my life to stay humble & hungry to evolve. I hope you enjoy my work and I'd love to hear your feedback.
- It's a great day to be alive!
Sensei Paul David

Scan & Follow/Like/Subscribe: Facebook, Instagram, YouTube: @senseipublishing

Scan using your phone/iPad camera for social media
Visit us at www.senseipublishing.com and sign up for our newsletter to learn more about our exciting books and to experience our FREE Guided Meditations for Kids & Adults.

www.ingramcontent.com/pod-product-compliance
Lightning Source LLC
Chambersburg PA
CBRC090901080526
44587CB00008B/163